AS TRUE AS THE BARNACLE TREE

Wherein:
Some tales from the old herbals are related, with a brief account of the Indian, Quaker, and Shaker usages of beneficial plants.

To which is added:
A short description of Catskill Mountains herb lore, a suggested plan for a herb garden, a listing of culinary herbs, and a sprinkling of herbal recipes.

Written and illustrated by Anita M. Smith (1893–1968), Herb Lady of the Catskills, with woodblock print by Maud and Miska Petersham on the front cover.

ANITA M. SMITH

WoodstockArts
Woodstock, New York

The publishers would like to thank Mary Petersham Reinhard
for granting permission to include artwork by her grandparents,
Maud and Miska Petersham; Jane Broderick for her editing;
and Abigail Sturges for the book design.

ISBN 978-0-9977164-2-9
Library of Congress Control Number: 2024938896
Printed and bound in the USA
Published by WoodstockArts
P.O. Box 1342
Woodstock, NY 12498
Tel: 845-679-8111
Email: info@woodstockarts.com
Visit: www.woodstockarts.com

CONTENTS

INTRODUCTION / 7

CHAPTER 1
OF DIVERSE HERBS AND THEIR USAGE / 15

CHAPTER 2
INDIAN HERB LORE / 23

CHAPTER 3
QUAKERS AND SHAKERS / 29

CHAPTER 4
WOODSTOCK LEGENDS AND CURES / 33

CHAPTER 5
SUGGESTED PLAN FOR A HERB GARDEN / 41

CHAPTER 6
FAVORITE CULINARY HERBS / 43

SELECTED SOURCES / 55
INDEX / 59
ABOUT THE AUTHOR / 66

INTRODUCTION

In 1939, when Anita M. Smith independently published *As True as the Barnacle Tree*, her herb business was six years old and booming. At that time, Smith was a sturdy woman in her early fifties with a sunny attitude and a soft spot for animals. Her faithful Scottie, Jackie Playboy Smith, was at her side as she potted seedlings in cold frames, picked bundles of herbs, and waited on customers. Her herb business, Stonecrop Garden & Shop, on lower Meads Mountain Road in Woodstock, New York, drew customers from all forty-eight contiguous states and was open from one pm to six pm daily—except Tuesdays—during the summer.

On the weekends, Woodstock residents such as Mr. and Mrs. Albert Cashdollar, the Town Supervisor and his wife, could be found browsing for garden ornaments. They might be seen talking with Mrs. Marion Bullard, the Woodstock correspondent for the Kingston *Daily Freeman*. Or one might find Mr. and Mrs. Leon Carey, the Town Clerk and his wife, hobnobbing there with the artist couple Konrad and Florence Ballin Cramer. Other customers included Georges Barrère, a classical flutist; Wilna Hervey, star of the Toonerville Trolley silent films; and Eugene and Elsie Speicher, one of the country's leading portrait painters and his wife. Customers were pleased to find the latest copy of the *Ulster County Townsman* at the checkout register; this was the kind of established business that offered such amenities.

Smith's herb shop was a gray clapboard building that featured all manner of herbs and sundries for the garden. One newspaper described the shop in a Sunday feature article:

> [It is] reminiscent of Dickens, with the bay window in front arrayed with a collection of gayly painted gourds, bundles of dried herbs, ornamental lanterns, leaden rabbits and decoy ducks for garden decorations, potpourri of Windsor rose in hand-turned pottery jars, old fashioned apothecary jars filled with spice, fennel seed, poppy seed, [and] sesame, which recalls to us the story of Ali Baba and the Forty Thieves. [There are also] spearmint and small jars of herbs for stews.
>
> There are more jars of intriguing shapes and sizes stored in the glass-doored cupboards, and when these doors are opened, a delicious combination of aromatic herbs fills the air.
>
> In the rear part of the shop, there is a storeroom which is every bit as fascinating to explore as the shop itself. From the old hand-hewn beams in the ceiling hang innumerable bunches of dried herbs and more strings of painted gourds. The walls of the room are lined with rustic birdhouses made by Woodstockers. [There are] handmade hearth brooms, more jars of herbs and jellies, garden tools, aprons, sundial faces, hand-wrought iron foot scrapers mounted on blocks of native bluestone, and almost everything else the garden-minded individual can think of.

As Anita Smith's business prospered, she began to purchase old herbals such as John Gerard's *The Herball or Generall Historie of Plantes*, 1633; Joseph Pitton de Tournefort's *The Compleat Herbal or The Botanical Institutions of M. Tournefort*, 1719; and Nicholas Culpeper's *English Physician and Complete Herbal*, 1813. Based on her study of these, she devised proprietary recipes for the new mixes of potpourri and herb-infused jams, jellies, and oils introduced in her shop each year.

She also drew on her research to write and illustrate the opening chapters of *As True as the Barnacle Tree*. Later chapters included the herbal practices of Native Americans, Catskill Mountain folk, and Quakers and Shakers. The book was set by hand and was one of the last to be printed and bound at Hervey White's Maverick Press. One purchaser of *Barnacle Tree* wrote on a postcard, "I am sending this booklet on to my daughter-in-law in Argentina, hoping to interest her in this cult. I used to have a large herb garden, but now have not room for it. Also, my husband does not care for the various nuances of flavoring. That makes a difference!"

With the shop's success, Smith was invited to speak several times on Kingston's WKNY. One of her radio scripts begins:

> The use of medicinal herbs and spices goes back to antiquity. The Bible has various references to herbs such as cassia, cinnamon, rue, hyssop, wormwood, and mandrake. Every good housewife in the Middle Ages had her kitchen garden full of herbs and spices for flavor and aroma. Therein would be a still room where she extracted oils for the perfumes and pomades, where the potpourri was mixed, and where she could dry the herbs for teas and infusions.

In notes for another radio program, she explains how Stonecrop Garden & Shop came to be:

> Well, I arrived in Woodstock as an artist, and it was really the Depression that made me change my career. People with a color sense are supposed to be keen on taste. Anyway, many of the artists in Woodstock are excellent cooks. Along with the others, I tried to give my friends good dishes and found it necessary to grow a few herbs for culinary purposes. As an enthusiastic gardener and with the increasing

> need to economize, perhaps it was natural that I would eventually use my experience to grow herbs for profit.

In the fall of 1940, a reporter from the New York *Herald Tribune* stopped by her shop and later wrote:

> In the shadow of Overlook Mountain, Woodstock, there is a garden, not of flowers but of herbs, whose fragrant spices are wafted by mountain breezes, where Miss Anita Smith, known as the Herb Lady of the Catskills, cultivates the plants from which she makes her living in one of the most unusual enterprises in New York State.

The article went on to note that Smith had finished harvesting her first herb crop from her acre of land, but, due to bad weather, she would only be able to get one more harvest instead of her usual three. Among the one hundred herbs under cultivation, she had ten different kinds of mint, a type of basil "immortalized in Keats's poem 'Isabella,' purple basil, and Tulasi, or Holy Basil of the Hindus."

In December of that year, Stonecrop Garden & Shop exhibited its products at the Eleventh Southern New York and Connecticut Antique Show in White Plains. Speaking invitations poured in from women's and garden clubs the following year. Press notices appeared in papers from around the area: Woodstock, Kingston, Rhinebeck, Accord, Poughkeepsie, Binghamton. *The Press and Sun-Bulletin* of Binghamton headlined a story "Herb Lady of the Catskills Speaks at Meeting."

The national recognition conferred by the New York *Herald Tribune* article attracted the attention of large companies like H. J. Heinz. The latter invited Smith to become a contract supplier of herbs and spices. However, she declined this honor as it would have required her to meet a monthly quota that she felt unable to fulfill.

♦ ♦ ♦

The Woodstock journey of Anita M. Smith (AMS) began in 1912 when she arrived in town with money intended for a ball gown. She planned to study painting at the well-known Arts Students League. She was a Quaker but also a refugee from the social whirl of Philadelphia's Main Line: Smith yearned to escape high society and devote her life to art. She had previously studied under William Merritt Chase and now took lessons from the leading landscape artist of the day, John F. Carlson. She rented the rustic Hanson Studio on Rock City Road near the four-corner intersection of Glasco Turnpike with Meads Mountain Road, and she took her meals at Rosie Magee's boarding house on the northeast corner.

By 1920, Smith had befriended Mr. and Mrs. Ashley Cooper, who had a farm in nearby Lake Hill. They sold her a piece of land on which she constructed a house. From Mrs. Cooper and another local farming woman, Mrs. Shultis, Smith learned how to put up and store vegetables for the winter. Although she continued to paint, her attention was increasingly drawn to the history of the land. On long winter evenings, AMS sat with farmers' wives while they quilted, and she listened to their stories about witches and skirmishes with bears and panthers. Out of these gatherings, Anita wrote a series of papers titled "Hearsay and History" for the Historical Society of Woodstock.

With the passing in 1928 of her mother, Lucy Pancoast Smith, AMS became independently wealthy and was determined to get back on track with her painting. But while she was traveling through southern France and the Pyrenees of northern Spain, pursuing her art, a family emergency interrupted her journey. Her sister, Frieda, was gravely ill in Woodstock, so Anita returned to her home in Lake Hill. While Frieda recovered, Anita cared for her sister's three small boys.

As a result of this family circumstance, as well as the onset of the Great Depression, AMS gradually turned her back on art and instead embraced gardening. From her time with the farmers' wives, she had learned about the healing properties of native plants. She began to experiment with herbs in her cooking. She extended dinner invitations to artist friends such as Zulma Steele, Julia Leaycraft, and Arnold and Lucile Blanch. Many of these artists had traveled to France and acquired an appreciation for herb-infused cooking. They so enjoyed Smith's cuisine that they encouraged her to develop a business with herbs. AMS turned the rocky ledges at the front of her Lake Hill home into a gardenscape of flowing color. Soon, her friends were asking for seedlings. In 1933, her hobby became a commercial enterprise, initially called Stonecrop Garden. She specialized in alpine, rock, and wildflower potted plants and began advertising in *The Overlook*.

Smith's old friend Rosie Magee had also died in 1928, and land from her farm at the four corners became available for sale. AMS purchased a four-acre parcel. She hoped Rosie would be glad to know that her apple trees were being well cared for by Anita. AMS constructed a stone cottage on this land. She later purchased a small building on Ohayo Mountain and had it conveyed to the lower end of her new property to serve as "a herb shop." (Smith always pronounced herb with the "h," in the cultured British way as opposed to the Cockney, with the h's dropped.)

During the Second World War, AMS erected an airplane spotter post adjacent to her herb-growing field, and she became

Woodstock's Chief Observer. In 1946, at the behest of James T. Shotwell, she began compiling a database of all the Woodstockers who had served their country in both world wars—to document Woodstock's role in these conflicts. In 1947 Anita was still running the flower table at the Woodstock Library Fair, but by 1955 she was hard at work writing Woodstock's first official history, *Woodstock History and Hearsay* (published in 1959; WoodstockArts issued a second edition in 2006).

Weston Blelock and Julia Blelock
Stonecrop
Woodstock, New York
March 2024

CHAPTER ONE

OF DIVERSE HERBS AND THEIR USAGE

The use of herbs is an ancient practice. We Americans have been negligent in herb usage. In the Bible, there are various references to herbs. However, in Genesis, Chapter One, where one finds, "And God said, Behold, I have given you every herb bearing seed," the reference is to the broader meaning of herbs as any plant whose stem is not woody. The division is between trees and shrubs on the one hand and herbs—including all grains—on the other. We now refer to herbs as fragrant plants that are beneficial for medicinal or culinary purposes. The Bible references such herbs as cassia, cinnamon, cumin, rue, hyssop, wormwood, mandrake, and those sweet odors of frankincense and myrrh. How beautiful is this quotation from the Song of Solomon: "Awake, O north wind; and come, thou south; blow upon my garden, that the spices thereof may flow out."

Herbs were closely identified with alchemy during the Dark Ages. There was also a belief that herbs were under the influence of the stars. In Nicholas Culpeper's work, each herb is listed according to its astrological influence. However, John Evelyn, writing in 1699, advises against consulting the governing planets and recommends instead that one look upon the plants themselves and judge their virtue by their complexions. Evelyn had much of the spirit of our times and has been called the "Patron Saint of the Salads." He says in his

Acetaria: A Discourse of Sallets that one acre of ground is sufficient to furnish and entertain a man's time and thoughts all his life long, with most innocent, agreeable, and useful employment. On another page may be read the pleasant adage that he who has bread and herbs is sufficiently blessed with all a frugal man could need or desire.

John Gerard's first herbal was published in 1597; in it, he gives a long account of those earlier herbalists to whom he is indebted, beginning with the ". . . wisest of men, even King Solomon, who certainely would not have medled with this subject, if he in his wisdom had not knowne it worthy himself, and exceeding fitting: First for the honor of his Creator, whose gifts and blessings these are: Secondly for the good of his Subjects, whereof without doubt, he in this worke had a speciall regard in the curing of their diseases and infirmities." And thus, it is with singular modesty that Gerard begins his *Herball or Generall Historie of Plantes.* Modern writers may show how much his herbal took from his predecessors, but we are grateful to him for the wisdom of writing for posterity that which became enriched by his telling. We acclaim him if only for these words: ". . . for it would be unseemly . . . for him that doth looke upon and handle faire and beautiful things to have his mind, not faire." Gerard (1545–1612) lived in an age that was beginning to doubt the truth of many miracles concerned with nature; he mocks the legend of the Mandragora and many others but does not doubt the truth of the Barnacle Tree. He says the latter existed along the coast of Lancashire, ". . . certaine trees whereon do grow certaine shells of a white colour tending to russet, wherein are contained little living creatures: which shells in time of maturitie do open, and out of them grow those little living things, which falling into the water do become fowles, which we call Barnacles; in the North of England, brant Geese; and in Lancashire, tree Geese: but the other that do fall upon the land perish and come to nothing." We are indebted to Gerard for the tale, as well as for a picture that inspired the drawing on the title page of this book.

John Parkinson, in his *Theatrum Botanicum* (1640), merely mentions the Barnacle Tree to scorn it, but he tells of other wondrous things. There is the Fountain Tree, whose leaves drip water continuously, enveloping the tree in a thick mist or cloud. It is supposed to grow in the Canary Islands, which would otherwise be without a source of fresh water. Another is the Sorrowful Tree, which hangs its leaves and sweet-scented blossoms in a withering aspect before the sun. The tree is supposed to contain the spirit of the fair daughter of a nobleman; once upon a time, the sun loved, deflowered, and abandoned her, so evermore the Sorrowful Tree shrinks from the sun's gaze.

Parkinson is more skeptical of the Dragon Tree, though he relates Pliny the Elder's story of its gum being the blood of a dragon or serpent crushed in combat with an elephant. He describes other fabulous herbage, such as the Scythian Lamb, which grows from a seed like a melon. It develops into a leafless stalk, atop which is a fruit resembling a young lamb with its head and legs hanging down. The rind or coat is wooly like a lamb's skin, but the flesh underneath is like that of a lobster. It feeds upon the grass immediately surrounding it, which, if removed, causes it to die.

Herba amoris is like the Sensitive Plant, which shrinks at the touch of a man. It has various medicinal attributes and is said to cause sleep when applied to the head—though sooner to an Indian [Native American] than a European. It was claimed by one physician of good credit that the possessor of this herb could have any woman he desired. To offset this, another observer claims for it the power to restore virgins who have been deflowered. This brings us to the virtues of the Chaste Making Tree of the West Indies, which the Indians would not allow to be burned, believing that whoever was touched by the flame or merely the smoke would become impotent.

Other strange remedies were used in olden times. Parkinson gives a long dissertation on the medicinal value of the "Mumme," meaning the body of a man or woman preserved with cedria and niter. He says that taken with a " . . . decoction of Marjerome, [it] helpeth a cough," taken "in drinke," it is a cordial for the heart, and in goat's milk it is very profitable against palsies, cramps, and so on down to lameness in the feet caused by cold and wet.

Gerard tells of Mumia, and Culpeper recommends that it be taken with dock and madder roots in red wine as an antidote for various ailments. Another rather gruesome cure of the sixteenth century was the moss that grew on dead men's skulls. Parkinson provides a vivid illustration and says, "it groweth upon the bare scalpes of men and women that have lyen long, and are kept in Charnell houses in divers Countries . . . to make the Unguentum Sympatheticum, which cureth wounds," and then adds, ". . . as Crolius hath it, It should be taken from the skulls of those who have been hanged or executed for offences."

If anyone should cringe at the foregoing descriptions, they should learn of some of the extraordinary early-American remedies, which include this cure for epilepsy: Take the left hind foot of an elk, because this animal being subject to those disorders removes them by scratching his ear with this hoof. The remedial hoof that is chosen should be black, very smooth and bright, and from it a decoction is made suitable for the sufferers to use.

A cure for stiff joints is the oil of fish worms, and the Eclectics were said to make use of frogs, poisonous snakes, and so on. There is a quaint custom of telling children that babies come from the

Digging Mandragora

knotty protuberances on the mulberry tree. They are told that if they chop these knobbles hard enough, they may uncover a baby—but, of course, by the time they are old enough to wield an axe efficiently they have learned better.

In ancient times, love philters were made of many herbs. One of the most famous plants used in witchcraft was Datura stramonium, whose seeds are given by sorcerers to cause fantastic visions and thieves to stupefy their victims. It is certainly a strong narcotic poison, as are henbane, mescal bean, hound's tongue, hemp, and mandragora, to mention but a few that have been used to break people's will. The use of mandragora goes back to antiquity; the ancients used it to reduce sensibility before surgery, and it was then held in high esteem. Because of its use as a love philter and in surgery, it came into ill repute, and there are many fables woven from the fact that its roots sometimes grew in the semblance of the human form. While being dug up, it reputedly shrieked in protest and even cast fatal spells. Shakespeare writes, "And shrieks like mandrakes torn out of the earth / That living mortals, hearing them, run mad." Of course, gatherers of such vicious herbs could demand an enormous price, and undoubtedly they kept the reputation alive. Some related how they were obliged to tie dogs to the herb to pull it forth to its death or to resort to other charms to offset the mandrake's spell.

Angelica root is one of those used against enchantments, and no harm may come to the man who carries it with him. Shepherds are reported to withstand evil spirits by twining bittersweet around their necks, and anise, verbena, and squill likewise work against spells. Mistletoe cut from a pear tree is also a remedy for witchcraft—but must not touch the ground after it is gathered. The leaves of herb Paris, called "True Love," were taken to restore those made foolish by witchcraft—though others tell of its use as an aphrodisiac.

Gerard quotes Lucius Apuleius Madaurensis, saying, "If Crowfeet [Ranunculus aquatilis] . . . be hanged in a linnen cloath about the necke of him that is lunaticke, in the waine of the moone, when the signe shall be in the first degree of Taurus or Scorpio, that then he shall forthwith be cured."

It is most comforting to find there are many more herbs that are beneficial than those that are harmful. Pliny reports that whosoever taketh the seed of rocket before he be whipped shall easily endure the pain. White ash is so offensive to reptiles that hunters have only to stuff their boots with its leaves to find immunity from rattlesnakes. Rue is said by Pliny to promote love in a man and diminish it in a woman. Cumin as a love potion is used to prevent fickleness. In one of the earliest English books on herbs, *The Grete Herball*, we are told,

"And for them that have melancolyike humours in theyr body / lete them ete borage with theyr flesshe or in theyr potage."

For a student, mint is a good herb to smell often. The lowly parsnip counteracts stupidity, and there are several others, such as pennyroyal and basil, to quicken the brain. However, basil might be dangerous for a scholar, as it has been used in love charms. Above all, the student is warned against using saffron, for if taken in large quantities it occasions involuntary mirth! Perhaps it is more costly than most condiments, but this is understandable when one considers that it is derived from the stigmas of Crocus sativus and it requires thousands of bulbs to produce a single ounce. Saffron has been famed since Biblical times for its scent and dye as well as for its flavor. As it is said in the Song of Solomon, "Spikenard and saffron; calamus and cinnamon, with all trees of frankincense; myrrh and aloes, with all the chief spices: A fountain of gardens, a well of living waters, and streams from Lebanon." *The Grete Herball* was first printed in 1526 by Peter Treveris. The following quotation is from a later copy; it is given as an example of the quaint old language we have been perusing. "Agaynst lytargye or forgetfulnesse [provoke] snesynge with castoreum / for it moeveth and comforteth [your] brayne. Or make comfeccyion of castoreum of mybtes / & [juice] of rew with vyneygre / & [shave] [your] heed / & rubbe [your] hyndre parte of the heed therewith."

A simpler aid to memory is to inhale the fragrance of rosemary, which has so many charms and virtues that they cannot all be enumerated. It is said to comfort the brain and one's sight; placed under the pillow, it keeps one from evil dreams. To drink a concoction of the leaves and flowers brings one to a merry mind, and drunk with thyme it is recommended for passions of the heart.

There are teas galore for soothing nerves, of which we suggest using sage or balm, vervain, chamomile, or mint. The cotton or down on quinces, boiled in wine and made up with wax, will, when applied to a bald scalp, bring hair back again.

As we bid the wayfarer goodbye, we can do no better than to hand him a sprig of mugwort, Artemisia vulgaris, the herb of travelers. Gerard writes: "Pliny saith, that the traveller or wayfaring man that hath the herbe tied about him feeleth no wearisomnesse at all; and that he who hath it about him can be hurt by no poysonsome medicines, nor by any wilde beast, neither yet by the Sun it selfe."

Freehand Drawing from The Grete Herball

CHAPTER TWO

INDIAN HERB LORE

When the settlers came to America, they discovered many strange plants and trees the Indians were using. Perhaps the most valuable to the Europeans for food were pumpkins, maize, beans, maple trees for their syrup, and potatoes. The Indians taught the white colonists of New England how to extract sap from the hard maples for sugar. One of my Quaker ancestors, fleeing religious persecution, came with his wife and infant son to Pennsylvania in 1682 to take possession of a tract of land in the wilderness. For weeks they lived in a cave where they would have perished if it had not been for the friendly Indians who gave them some of their stores of pumpkins and peas and helped them to construct a wigwam, where they lived until it was possible to build a more comfortable house. Meanwhile, the Indians taught them how to raise their own corn and pumpkins, which they grew the following summer, and thereafter all went well.

The northern Indians did not cultivate many plants. They were known to have grown corn, beans, pumpkins, sunflowers, and tobacco. The only fruit said to have been planted by them was plum, although they gathered wild cherries, apples, and berries, including cranberries, along with the natural herbage, which they cooked with their game. They collected wild seeds in abundance—rice, flax, dill, acorns, and chinquapins. And, of course, they gathered and consumed many roots; several examples are Medeola virginiana, the Indian cucumber; jack in the pulpit, called Indian turnip; and Indian "potatoes," glycine apios, whose roots resembled those of actual potatoes. The Quaker John Bartram related that some Indians ate not only these tubers but also the peas that lie in the pods of this plant, which they prepared like common peas.

For medicinal purposes, the Indians used innumerable barks, roots, berries, and leaves. They often dried, pounded, and mixed these with the fats of wild animals, the liquid tapped from trees, or mineral spring waters. They would gorge themselves when food was plentiful, and if they became uncomfortable they used medicinal herbs or, in some cases, earth that was later found to contain magnesium. Among the herbs and trees they used for cures were the American mandrake, milkweed, boneset—called Joe-Pye weed after an Indian of that name—jimsonweed, bearberry, bloodroot, feverfew, lobelia (also used in love charms), spikenard, witch hazel, pine, sassafras, peach, arbutus, gentian (nicknamed Indian quinine), sumac, black cohosh (called squawroot), and wintergreen, to name some that grew in New York State. From southern tribes, the Indians acquired their chief tonics, which were sarsaparilla and cinchona. The rough stone mortar and pestles they left behind are to be seen in many museums. They also pounded their food in the trunks of hardwood logs made by burning and scooping one end until a hollow was made for a bowl.

The common life everlasting of our fields was a plant much used by the Indians and carried by their medicine men. It is slightly sedative when slept upon, is good for the throat when smoked (both Parkinson and Gerard recommend it for quinsy), and one writer even claims it will not only clear the voice but create a desire to sing. Another name for it is cudweed—the word derived, according to Joseph Pitton de Tournefort, from the custom of giving it to cattle that have lost their ruminating faculty. Perhaps it is the herb that induces cows so often to turn their heads away from all the beauty of the pastures to spend hours facing tree trunks to chew their cuds. Fortunately, there is no danger that everlasting will make them break into song, no matter what effect it may have had on the indigenous people.

The Indians used various herbs to help withstand fatigue. They smoked henbane for this purpose. Henbane, or Indian hemp, was also used in the tropics by priests and enchanters to gain control of their victims. The cattail flag root was chewed while on journeys to allay thirst and provide nourishment.

Perhaps the northern Indians were too fatalistic to attempt to make nature do their bidding by planting seeds; more often, they merely gathered the harvest offered them from the wilderness. When they did plant a few crops, they allowed nature to take her course, and if diseases or insects damaged the plants, they considered the failure due to evil spirits. In "The Song of Hiawatha," Longfellow describes the beautiful ceremony of blessing the cornfields by having Minnehaha disrobe in the dark silence of the night and walk barefoot around the fields:

> "You shall bless to-night the cornfields . . .
> Thus the fields shall be more fruitful,
> And the passing of your footsteps
> Draw a magic circle round them,
> So that neither blight nor mildew,
> Neither burrowing worm nor insect,
> Shall pass o'er the magic circle . . . "

Later, when Hiawatha was filled with melancholy by the drowning of Chibiabos, there came a visit from the medicine men, the Medas, to appease and console him with magic roots and "simples." They gave him a magic drink made of spearmint and yarrow, roots of power, and herbs of healing. They shook their medicine pouches over his head, and straightaway from his brain departed his melancholy mood.

M. R. Gilmore, in a paper written for the Bureau of American Ethnology, mentions ginseng, one of our most famous local roots, as having been used in Pawnee love charms. It was mixed with red columbine seed, cardinal flowers, and seeds of Cogswellia daucifolia (wild carrot). To carry this charm combined with a few hairs from the head of the one desired would make the possessor irresistible. Seeds of wild carrot alone, carried in a pocket, would make a person attractive to anyone.

Peyote, sometimes called mescaline, is commonly used among the Indians of the Southwest and Mexico, for whom it has religious significance. It has narcotic properties and will induce visions, as well as extraordinary sensations of exaltation, along with a lapse of the awareness of time.

Gilmore describes a taboo among the Indians regarding digging the roots of wild gourd vines, for fear of bringing calamity or even death. However, certain authorized persons might dig it with offerings of tobacco, accompanied by prayers to the spirit of the plant. When acquired from others, the roots were prized for their medicinal virtues; Gilmore explains that this was according to the doctrine of signatures, since the root was said to resemble the human form and to be male and female. As a remedy, the portion of the root used was that which corresponded to the location of the ailment in the human. It is interesting to compare this belief with a similar tradition in the Old World regarding mandragora.

The narrow-leaved purple coneflower is another plant used by the Indians as a medicine. Gilmore relates that a Winnebago told him

Indian Garden

he had often used the plant to make his nerves insensible to heat so he could take live coals in his mouth. The juice is likewise used by Indians of many tribes for burns, and magicians are supposed to have applied it to their hands and arms so that they might remove pieces of meat from pots of boiling water without harming themselves.

Parkinson tells of a herb from the West Indies that would stop the flow of blood from any wound. It is said that starving Indians were known to cut off the calves of their legs for food; by applying the leaves of this unnamed herb, it would immediately staunch the blood, to the great admiration of all who saw it. Wahoo comes from the bark of Euonymus atropurpureus and is known as an excellent tonic. The Indian medicine men employed it; they used this peculiar name when chanting their secret incantations. The sacred bark of their medicine bags was probably cascara sagrada.

In Father Noël Dumarest's notes on New Mexico, he includes an account of a herb that was given to sick Indians to terrify the witches that were supposed to "possess" them; witches were thought to cause not only illness but also evil. When a medicine man was called, he would give the patient Katshrana (a herb so named by the Cochiti tribe)—to be either smoked or ground and eaten. It had the reputation of being a medicinal remedy as well as a herb used to fumigate witches.

To conclude this brief history of Indian usage, it is pleasant to recall an account of an Iroquois meal described by John Bartram in his journal of 1743. The dinner consisted of hominy soup in which fish, young squash, and squash flowers had been boiled. Diners were also given dumplings of fresh, soft corn scraped from the cob, wrapped with beans, and cooked in corn leaves. Certainly, this was excellent provision.

CHAPTER THREE

QUAKERS AND SHAKERS

Every man under his vine and under his fig-tree

The Pilgrims brought to America many of the seeds for their cottage gardens, including thyme, marjoram, savory, mint, parsley, and chives, with chamomile and sage for tea and perhaps a dozen other herbs precious to the kitchen and the medicine chest. The first real physic garden in America is said to have been in the botanic plantings of the Quaker John Bartram. After searching the entire colony for native plants and trees, he began his garden in Philadelphia circa 1728. Thereafter, the Quakers were diligent in their study and use of herbs, and it is said that agriculture flourished wherever there were settlements of Friends. In one Quaker garden planted along the Delaware River, a fine planting of herbs remained until the early 1900s. From an account given to us by Miss Julia Abbott, we can recreate the pattern of that "Friend's" kitchen yard. There were mint, thyme, catnip, and chives for the borders. There were sage for stuffing, marjoram and basil for flavoring, and chamomile for a stimulating tea. Lavender was placed among the linens to keep away moths. There was a clump of comfrey, whose sticky roots were mashed with salt pork for bruises and for wounds. This is the Symphytum officinale, whose use goes back to ancient times and is said to be so healing that if its roots are boiled with cut flesh, it will consolidate the separate pieces. In this garden, there was horehound to be boiled with molasses and tar for colds and spikenard for its aromatic roots. From the last, an extract was taken for perfume and used for burial spices, a custom that dates to Biblical times.

There was also cinquefoil to be made into campfire tea for all the ills that flesh is heir to. To allay inflammation, there were smartweed, heartsease, and jimsonweed (Datura stramonium), from which poultices were made. Handy by, burdock and yellow dock were grown for their virtues as astringents. In the fields throughout were also mayapple, live-forever, boneset, wild carrot for the kidneys, wintergreen for rheumatism and dandelions to purify the blood, pennyroyal, and tansy for flavoring puddings. Back in the garden were foxglove and rue, that ancient emblem of sorrow called "herb of grace." It was said to be used against witchcraft, but to this a Quaker was reported to have added, "Of course we were Friends, and that was just hearsay." Next to the rue were planted vines of Balsam apple (Momordica balsamina). From this, a decoction was made by pouring whiskey over the apples; allowed to stand on the mantel for a few weeks, it was always ready to be used on cuts and sores. There were trees of dogwood, sassafras, and spicewood—used not only to purify the blood but also in the making of harvest beer. How fragrant this garden must have been, with its healing aromas, the gaiety of its flowering herbs, and the peace of a Quaker mistress to lovingly tend and gather her "simples"—not such a long while ago.

The first medicinal herbs grown commercially in this country were probably those raised by the Shakers. At one of their colonies in New Lebanon, New York, the Shakers ran a large industry—growing and gathering herbs and barks, which they macerated and distilled into extracts and medicines. Agriculture was exalted by the

Shakers to religious significance. In *The Shaker Manifesto* of 1878, they affirm that it was not the purpose of the church to gather or lay up an interest in worldly goods; they pledged to freely give their time and talents for the mutual good of one another and to use any surplus for charitable purposes. Ten years later they had laid out a kitchen garden, for the use of the "Family" at New Lebanon, of such proportions that they needed to appoint an "Orchard Deacon" for its management. This community was self-supporting into the early 1900s. As vegetarians, they could easily raise all their food, and they spun the cloth for their simple garments without recourse to outside commodities. What little they chose to buy was readily paid for by their own produce.

It was said that the difference between the Shakers and other farmers was that the latter were laboring only for profit while the Shakers were striving for service. Certainly, their industries prospered, and it was not long before the little Shaker wagons traveled far and wide, carrying extracts and medicines to an ever-widening circle. Everything that was bought with the Shaker stamp proved to be of full measure and value. It is said the Shakers were the first to sell seeds in little packets. In New Lebanon the Shakers produced many other goods, from furniture and pens to bonnets and brooms, but their seed and herb gardens were tremendous, and they sent their medicinals as far as London and Paris. By 1850, their records show, they were pressing 21,000 pounds of herbs, roots, and barks, and their physic garden covered fifty acres. They bottled tinctures by the thousands, extracts for flavoring, and even distilled rose water, verbena, and other sweet flowers—but never was a flower grown simply for pleasure. One Shaker woman relates that the flowers raised by the community were much admired by outsiders but the Sisters were convinced by training that a rose was useful, not ornamental. Certainly, they lived in all simplicity, helping each other and bringing up many orphans—although this was one way of acquiring converts, for all members were required to take an oath of celibacy. Life was most austere; the original Shakers had been recruited from among the Quakers by those who believed the Society of Friends was becoming far too worldly. They stripped from life the nonessentials, relinquishing all private possessions to rally under the banner of their founder, Mother Ann Lee, with their hands to work and their hearts to God.

CHAPTER FOUR

WOODSTOCK LEGENDS AND CURES

In the seventeenth century, when the Dutch landed along the Hudson River and looked up at the Onteoras, meaning "Blue Mountains," they heard from the Indians about the strange spirits that dwelt in the forest of hemlock and beech and among the swirling clouds that clung to the bluestone ledges. There were entities said to control the sunshine and the storms, while others identified themselves with the wild animals of the forests or took the forms of bubbling springs, playful deer, or mischievous boulders that might go thundering down the cloves between the hills.

Years later, the Dutch and English, with their spinning wheels and skillets, settled throughout the Catskills, as they now called the Blue Mountains. These were matter-of-fact folks who had to wrest a living from the rocky land and the harsh weather. They chopped down the mighty trees of the forests, drove the creeks to turn their gristmills, and shot the birds and beasts in the wood. All the while, the injured spirits of the mountains took their revenge by breaking nature's bonds with a terrific storm that might clatter its thunder around the peaks and incite each spring and rivulet to gush into tortuous activity, pouring exuberant streams downhill to boil into the creeks and over into the valleys.

Sometimes the evil spirits would take their toll by possessing a soul here or there, who would be only dimly aware of their kinship. I knew such a one, named Johannes, whose plight was recognized throughout the valley. He was a strong, bearded man and, when directed, could plow and reap and chop wood on his farm as well as anyone. He was kind and gentle, but while pursuing these ordinary tasks he lived an inner life of horror. His mind was under the domination of a voice from the mountains that was driving him ever harder. Poor man, he could never rest, for as soon as the day's chores were done, the tormenting voice took possession. Hundreds of taboos were laid upon him; for example, he dared not step upon the flagstones that led to the barn, chew tobacco bought from the local store, or work with certain neighbors. One winter, the voice ordered him to pump forth the water that resided in the well, and his family was tortured by the sounds of the senseless pumping until the water supply gave out. During the day, he was prevented from doing this, but when the household had gone to sleep, Johannes would heed the voice urging him to get out of bed and hurry to the well. Then, throughout the night, his family would hear the wheeze and glurk of the pump handle and the uneven rush of water pouring forth for no good purpose. Up behind the eaves, the frightened children would pull the covers over their heads as they shivered in bed. At last, the thirst of the voice seemed to be appeased—but only to give way to graver suggestions. Fear entered the surrounding farmhouses when night skies were reddened with leaping bonfires on the high knolls at the bidding of a spirit of which they had no ken. Fortunately, this urge also passed, and, finally, the voice told Johannes that the mountains would surely crash upon the people of the valley unless he piled up enough rocks to assuage their fury. Night after night, this driven soul could be heard at this task in the high pastures. All the loose stones were piled high in heap after heap, requiring ever more effort to build up, yet still the voice goaded him without mercy. When no more stones could be found nearby, Johannes tore at the cliffs with his bare hands. Sometimes the loose bluestone slabs could be pried out, and a weakened mass of ledge would crash down with volcanic clamor until the whole of the midnight valley reverberated to a thunderous noise, a tribute to the old witch spirits atop the Catskills.

Talking on winter evenings with older residents of the valley has brought forth many such tales of the souls claimed by mountain spirits. I have often retold the story of the old woman on Overlook who changed herself into a deer to leap about the cemetery and who could only be hurt by a silver bullet. Or the tale of the witch living near Indian Head Mountain who enchanted some piglets. Or the story of the old woman of Mink Hollow with one misshapen foot who could cast a spell by crying out, "Pocks-e-Rollins." This woman seemed like an ordinary neighbor most of the time, and she married and raised a large family. Trouble arose only when she was crossed, and then, with pride in her powers, she would invoke the help of the Devil. He would enable her to bewitch the wheels off a passing cart or fly miles through the night to cast a spell upon a distant farm or set a white cock to crowing in the dark to scare the wits from all who heard. Ordinary folks could get the best of her only by cutting a witch hazel branch, which was used frequently to "switch the witches out of her skirt tails."

Fortunately, there were also witch doctors who could be called upon. From the great-grandson of one of the best-known witch doctors, I learned of his horseshoe cure and his laying on of hands, which was usually accompanied by a medicinal pill. This witch doctor had a thriving practice from which he made a good living until a law was passed that prevented him from accepting fees for his services. Even so, he continued to travel through the countryside in his buggy—bringing succor to bedeviled souls, who, in their gratitude, gave him many gifts.

One of the most recent legends of Woodstock is the story of a young poet who, after a long walk, fell asleep in a deep valley. He awakened to hear the voice of the "little people," who had taken possession of the clearing in the woods where he lay. There are still people who can wield a witch hazel stick to help them find water; indeed, the best well in my neighborhood was located this way. To this day, there are descendants who tell of the young bride whose older husband was so jealous he beat her to death. She had gone to help a sick neighbor, so they say; when he came home drunk and couldn't find her, he cut himself an elm gad to await her return. He subsequently used this to such purpose that she was taken ill and never recovered. Before she died, she asked that the elm gad be buried with her, and in due course there grew from the grave a mighty elm tree. It dominated the sad place for many years.

The township of Woodstock runs through the valley along the southern slope of the Catskills from the foot of Overlook to Mount Tremper. Here, for one hundred and fifty years, people have written their history only upon the land from which it was so hard to earn a living. They were forced into other occupations besides farming; even if the homegrown produce fed them, it was necessary to turn elsewhere for cash. After the first forest trees were mercilessly felled for the tanneries and the second growth of saplings was cut for barrel hoops, many families still turned to the fields and woods for succor. There were two herbs that repaid the trouble taken to gather them; one of these was ginseng and the other was wintergreen. There was a distillery near Phoenicia where the essential oil of wintergreen was extracted for commerce, and whole families hunted the fields for the bright red berries with their pleasant taste.

Ginseng was the more valuable crop. In China, it was considered to be worth several times its weight in gold; its consumption was attributed to the longevity of some of the Chinese emperors. The leaves were used in tea, but the roots—supposed to resemble the human form—were thought to be the most efficacious part of the plant. The Chinese took recourse to it as a last remedy for almost any disease. The name is said to mean "wonder of the world," and the English name Panax comes from "panacea." Statistics from the year 1830 show that the export of these roots to China amounted to over 300,000 pounds. Orientals also used the roots of this herb as an aid to fertility, for which there was a constant demand. Ginseng grows best in the deep forests under beech and butternut trees and is about a foot high with umbels of four branches, to which are attached leaves similar in appearance to woodbine. In the center of the umbel grows a white flower cluster, which turns into red berries in the fall. It would be easier to find these bright berries if the chipmunks were not so fond of them. If the chipmunks eat them to encourage their fertility, this might account for the increase of one and the decrease of the other.

In Woodstock, there are persons still using the old medicinal herbs. Infusion of sweet fern is recommended for poison ivy. In one farmhouse, I found large bunches of this drying for tea, which is reputed to be excellent for rheumatism. One neighbor told me of a coffee made from parched rye grains, which, after being ground with a pestle, was boiled in a pot. Another showed me his bunch of "scouring rush" to be used for kidney troubles. One told of gathering puffballs to staunch the bleeding of wounds, and others have spoken of using spotted maple bark in making a spring tonic. Yarrow can be used to tone up the blood, and an infusion of dried mullein leaves will serve the same purpose. Boneset is for the stomach, with mayapple as a substitute for calomel, pennyroyal, sassafras, and golden seal, with cockerel, for croup. Arbutus was called gravel weed because of its use for kidneys, and as one old woman said, "We never thought of it as a flower." Old Mrs. Wagner of Willow told of giving her babies catnip tea to make them sleep: "Not a weed that grows that isn't good for something." For her children's bruises she would apply crushed plantain leaves. She made onions into an excellent poultice. For colds she made an onion syrup by covering slices of onion with sugar to simmer on the back of the stove until the juice was drawn out. Another syrup for colds was made by cooking together a cup of molasses, a stick of licorice, a pinch of cayenne, and a teaspoonful of butter. It was Mrs. Wagner, then nearly one hundred years old, who described how she had made vinegar from maple syrup. She boiled the sap down by half and allowed it to "spoil"; water was then added, and it would ferment, turning to vinegar. This, she said, must be kept in a warm place. On another farm one autumn, the housewife was found busy stirring the contents of a great iron kettle full of a not-unpleasant-smelling brew. Upon inquiry, she replied that she was "rendin' down" her catch of skunk fat to make ointment against winter colds.

Among the herbs to be found in the farm dooryards are parsley, sage, spearmint, and wormwood—but the old people usually gathered their "simples" from the wilds. Calling a doctor was costly and not always convenient. Many of the settlements counted upon local people to do their doctoring. In Mink Hollow, there lived "Aunt Phoebe," who for many years made healing poultices that were supposed to be far better than those given by the doctor. Another woman could cure cancer with sheep sorrel—or so it was said!

One hundred years ago, Betsey Booth, who lived back of Overlook, was famous for her Consumptive Syrup. She was a stalwart woman who thought nothing of walking to Saugerties or Kings-

The Herb Stall at Stonecrop

ton, a distance of fifteen miles, to do her "trading" and back again the same day with all her purchases. If it was winter, she would take a heated brick for warmth. She was a real feminist and was the first woman known to wear trousers in Woodstock. She would be seen picking wild strawberries in her husband's breeches, which was considered most daring. She was known all through the hills for her skill at doctoring, and for many years Aunt Betsey's concoctions brought comfort to the whole neighborhood. She gathered herbs and made infusions of sweet fern for fever and spearmint for the stomach, catnip and sage for the nerves, and gentian (called "blue-blows-stuff") for dysentery. Her best-known remedy was her syrup of sassafras for the lungs. Two of her sons served in the Civil War, and they used her remedies with such success that they would write home again and again asking their mother to send her "Cholera Syrup." Aunt Betsey would often stay up all night to tend her crocks of syrup simmering at the back of the stove; she would pack this up and send it south to the soldiers on the battlefields. The recipe for this syrup has been carefully guarded by her descendants and is still bringing comfort to the grandchildren in times of need. Betsey Booth, with her big heart, trekking over the mountains gathering herbs, tending the sick, and raising a large family, represents the best of a past generation of Woodstock.

CHAPTER FIVE

SUGGESTED PLAN FOR A HERB GARDEN

One function of a herb garden is to lighten melancholy and give an understanding heart to those who walk therein. Therefore, it is essential in planning a herb garden to have little walks, preferably of stone; between the slabs, thyme, Nepeta mussinii, or white violets can be planted. Chamomile will also work well, as it represents patience, and the more it is trodden upon the lustier its growth!

The path could be edged with a miniature hedge of rue or lavender or Artemisia or chives. Or, if desired, stones on edge would make a nice border with plants of flax set behind to fountain their sky-blue flowers along the fragrant route. On either side would be little beds of herbs for flavoring and perfume. The path should lead to a seat, preferably of stone, placed under a trim little fruit tree or shrub, and here one could linger to enjoy the pleasant outlook. Beneath the bench would be mints, grateful for the shade and refreshing to smell when they are bruised. Not far away should be an assembly of sweet geraniums for idle fingers to pinch—among them peppermint, rose, nutmeg, apple, and Pelargonium crispum, the most refreshingly spiced of them all. It would be nice to set the rosemary plants nearby, and a few old-fashioned roses, and behind them valerian and bee balm. These plants all stand separate, ranging around the seat to exhale sweet fragrance. Quite different are the horizontal masses of the beds of marjoram, thyme, French sorrel, borage, chervil, and soft horehound. In the middle distance would be stiff rows of thin herbs like dill and coriander and cumin, fennel, and rampion. Behind them would grow the coarser stalks of angelica and lovage, costmary and tansy. Near the paths and easy to reach should be beds of basil, parsley, savory, tarragon, and chives, for these are the favorite culinary herbs. Girdle the whole garden with a stone wall or a hedge of sweet-smelling shrubs. In one corner set a beehive, and somewhere else a rustic birdbath with a tiny rill, if possible, wherein to grow watercress and spearmint. Remember, always, that the garden tells the story of its owner's mind and heart.

Stonecrop Herb Garden

CHAPTER SIX

FAVORITE CULINARY HERBS

In Pottage without Herbs there is neither goodness nor nourishment.
—from the Physicians of Myddrai

B*asil*—Ocimum basilicum, under the influence of Mars and Scorpio, is an annual, easy to grow and indispensable for culinary uses. The popularity of this herb has waxed and waned with every age. Originally it was said to have been named after a king. Subsequently Aelius Galenus and Pedanius Dioscorides held it not fitting to be taken inwardly, although Pliny defends it. Culpeper attributes its virulent quality to its being under Scorpio. He quotes Mizaldus, "that if it be laid to rot in horse-dung, it will breed venomous beasts," and Hollerius, a French physician, affirming that an acquaintance, "by common smelling to it had a scorpion bred in his brain." But Simeon Zethy, writing in Latin, says that the "smell of Basill is good for the heart and for the head" and "maketh a man merry and glad," with which I agree. Ocimum sanctum is the holy basil or Tulasi of the Hindus, being consecrated to Vishnu, and a sprig is placed on the breast of their dead. To the living, it brings good fortune, and for that alone it should be planted, as well as for its invigorating odor.

Sweet basil and bush basil are both delicious in meat cookery, either fresh or dried. Fresh sprigs may be chopped and added to consommé just before serving, or to salads. It gives the special flavor to tomato dishes for which the Italians are famous.

Tomato Soup

After heating a can of tomato soup, pour it over a tablespoon of cottage cheese and sprinkle with chopped basil.

Borage—Borago officinalis, is an annual herb of Jupiter. "Borage brings always courage," Gerard tells us. "Pliny calleth it *Euphrosium*, because it maketh a man merry and joyfull." Gerard continues with a recommendation to use a cough syrup of borage with sugar, adding thereto the powder of the bones of a stag's heart against swoonings and the passions of the heart. We believe the desired results may be obtained by dropping the flower heads in a wine cup. Although it is rather untidy, blue borage is pretty enough to have its place in the herb garden. The leaves, when young, have a cucumber-like taste that is pleasant in salads.

Chervil, or sweet cicely—Anthriscus cerefolium, under the influence of Jupiter, has been called the "leaf which rejoyceth and comforteth the heart." It is a perennial, easy to grow and pleasant to look upon as well as to taste. It may be used wherever parsley is recommended. Parkinson claims the leaves, seeds, and roots are so fine and pleasant in salads that no other is comparable to it and it gives a better relish to any other herbs put with it. Gerard tells us, "The roots are likewise most excellent in a sallad, if they be boyled and after dressed as the cunning Cooke knoweth how better than myself: notwithstanding I doe used to eate them with oile and vinegar, being first boyled; which is very good for old people that are dull and without courage." Gerard further says that the plant is delicious but "increaseth lust." To the contrary, Tournefort claims that it produces "sweet sleep."

Chervil with tarragon and chives compose the "fines herbes" of the famous French omelets. It is also good sprinkled green on bouillon and gives a snappy tang to herb sandwiches.

Dill—Anethum graveolens, under the influence of Mercury, is in appearance like fennel. But it is an annual, though it frequently reseeds itself. Tournefort recommends it as a cure for hiccoughs, and, for the same malady, Parkinson says to take the seeds in wine. In this country, it is the invariable accompaniment to cucumber pickles. The flower umbels are agreeable in salads and are especially good sprinkled over summer squash.

Fennel—Foeniculum vulgare, governed by Mercury, is a slender, easily raised perennial growing about four feet high with umbels of yellow flowers soon followed by the seeds. Fennel was associated with sight in ages past and was frequently recommended to clear the eyes from mist and film. As John Evelyn suggests, "it sharpens the Sight and recreates the Brain." Tournefort attributes such virtue to these seeds steeped in vinegar with honey and cinnamon that he claims will recover sight to persons over eighty years of age in a manner most incredible. Altogether it must be a very valuable herb, for Parkinson, after recounting many virtues, advises its use "for those that are growen fat to abate their unweldinesse and make them more gaunt and lanke." It is also recommended for restoring color to the face. This is contrary to the attributes of its relative, cumin, whose seeds were eaten not only for their royal flavor but to create an interesting pallor to the complexion.

The stalks of fennel are boiled as a vegetable. The ordinary sweet fennel is grown for its seed and is especially recommended to be sprinkled over baked fish or ground into the white sauce. The flowers and leaves are a delicious addition to potato salad.

Oregano or Pot Marjoram—Origanum vulgare, under the influence of Mercury, is a dependable perennial with its lavender flowers and pleasant flavor. It grows about a foot high, may be placed behind the edging of other herbs, and will grow in poor soil. It is good to drop into stuffing, soup, and stews, and, being available early in the season, is welcome in herb sandwiches and salads.

Sweet Marjoram—Origanum majorana, more to our taste, is a delightful little annual no more than six inches high with a persuasive flavor. Culpeper says it is a herb of Mercury and therefore an excellent remedy for the brain. He, as well as Parkinson, claims that it "helpeth the losse of speech by the resolution of the tongue." Gerard recommends marjoram as a remedy against the stinging of venomous beasts, as a cure for those who have drunk opium, against the swoonings of the heart, and so on. Parkinson adds, "Our daintiest women doe put it to still among their sweet hearbs, to make sweet washing water."

It is delicious in soups and meat dishes. A ten-cent can of consommé, heated with a teaspoonful of chopped marjoram, chervil, and savory and poured over a slice of lemon to serve, is lifted far above the mediocre tinned soup to subtle excellence.

Mint—Mentha requienii, under Venus, is a perennial herb that is easy to grow and harder to keep from spreading. Culpeper quotes Pliny as saying that mint exhilarates the mind and is therefore proper for the studious. Pliny has also said that mint stirs up the taste to a speedy desire for meat.

This herb is given as a remedy for a dozen different diseases, but Culpeper warns against taking mint, since whoever eats it when wounded will never be cured. Gerard opens his discourse on mints with, "There be divers sorts of Mints; some of the garden; other wilde, or of the field; and also some of the water." There are about thirty distinct species of mint; here at Stonecrop, we grow ten, and each variety has its following. The leaves of some are downy, some are round, and others are long and dark.

For juleps, the favorite is the Russian or curly mint, although apple mint runs close behind in popularity for drinks. Peppermint is the choice for mint sauce, and spearmint and orange mint are also in demand, the latter being especially good in iced tea. There is also a miniature creeping mint. Most of the mints like wet ground but will do well on upland soil.

Onion family—Allium, under Mars, includes onions, chives, and shallots, indispensable to fine cuisine. Onions are necessary for soups and stews, chives make for successful green salads, and shallots are a refinement of the garlic flavor that figures largely in French casserole recipes. The herbalists of old thought more of onions for their medicinal value than for flavor. John Evelyn waxes indignant at the thought of garlic, which he absolutely forbids in his "Salleting, by reason of its intolerable Rankness, and which made it so detested of old; that the eating of it was part of the Punishment for such as had committed the horridest Crimes."

He continues, "To be sure, 'tis not for Ladies Palats, nor those who court them, farther than to permit a light touch on the dish." Gerard recommends the juice of onions to anoint bald heads in the sun to bring again the hair very speedily. Onions or garlic put in mole runs are supposed to drive them forth—but, as with the bad penny, we fear they may appear elsewhere and do greater harm. Parkinson tells us the country people of England hold that the eating of onions is preventative of infection. Certainly, through the ages all peoples have used onion poultices to good advantage.

Herb Sandwich

Chop fresh sprigs of chives, tarragon, parsley, fennel, marjoram, and rosemary into a bowl with several radishes. Mix in a tablespoon of mayonnaise dressing, salt, pepper, and a few drops of herb vinegar. This is a very refreshing summer sandwich filling.

Parsley—Petroselinum crispum, under Mercury, is usually treated as an annual. This well-known herb is too often considered a garnish rather than an integral flavor for soups and salads.

The Hamburg or root parsley is very hardy and useful for its roots when dried. It is also valuable for its second-year growth, as it becomes ready to use early in the season. When it has gone to flower and seed, the umbels are delicious to mix into mayonnaise. Chopped parsley mixed with butter and a few drops of lemon juice makes a good sauce for broiled fish. Curly parsley is a fragrant appetizer and a charming garland to encircle the herb garden.

Gerard quotes Pliny, saying that "the leaves are pleasant in sauces," and "they be also singular good to take away stoppings, and to promote urine: which thing the roots likewise do notablie performe if they be boiled in broth: they be also delightfull to the taste, and agreeable to the stomacke." Parsley was used as a garland herb to crown the victors at the Greek games. Gerard further claims that parsley roots or seeds boiled in ale "and drunken, cast forth strong venome or poison." The modern association of parsley and drinking is the use of one to cover up the breath of the other.

Rosemary—Rosmarinus officinalis, a herb of which Culpeper says, "The Sun claims privilege in it, and it is under the Celestial Ram."

The herbal of Monsieur Tournefort, chief botanist to Louis XIV, was translated into English in 1719. He describes rosemary as an "Under-shrub of a most delicious Scent, smelling like Incense very well known by reason of its usefulness, and has got the name of Coronarius, because it is much used in Garlands. It flowers early in Spring, and almost the whole Summer over. The Flowers break forth from the Wings of the Leaves, being of whitish blue Colour." Later, he continues, the "Smoak and Vapour of this Plant in Plague-time, cures the Air and renders it wholesome . . . The Plant dried and cut, and smoaked like Tobacco, is reckoned to have great Efficacy in a Cough . . . They make Combs in

France of thick Trunks . . . with which they who desire to be preserved from a Giddiness, comb their Heads every Day." Again, "If the Flowers or Leaves be boiled with Wine and Honey . . . and taken before going to Sleep it is of wonderful Effect toward curing of Asthma and clearing the Voice." Culpeper goes one step further and says this herb is good for a dull and melancholy man, and the powder of the flowers bound on the right arm with a linen cloth will work into the veins and make a man more merry than ordinary.

In modern times, rosemary is still surrounded by romance. Certain members of a family to whom I have presented bouquets of herbs are especially fond of the taste of rosemary. Unfortunately, they could never detect the flavor of this herb in their food, though they were given numerous sprigs of it. At last, it was revealed that their Hungarian cook had removed and potted every bit in the belief that she would catch a husband if she could succeed in rooting rosemary.

In this climate rosemary will not live over the winter unless potted for the kitchen window. It is a prime flavor when sprinkled over roasts or fowl and is an important addition to stews.

Sage—Salvia officinalis, under Jupiter, is a hardy perennial, thought to be beautiful for its flowers and foliage. The most beloved herb of Anglo-Saxons, it is famous for its predominant flavor in sausage and sauce for veal and duck—although a little goes a long way for some of us. Tournefort describes it as a very wholesome plant, but he advises us to wash it carefully since toads frequently nestle under it. To keep away the toads, Italians are wont to plant rue intermixed with sage. If this is done, sage taken with salt while fasting is said to keep one safe from the bites and poison of any venomous creature. Culpeper claims that sage is an aphrodisiac. To Evelyn, "in

Sketch for the Cover of a Stonecrop Brochure

short, 'tis a Plant endowed with so many and wonderful Properties, as the assiduous use of it is said to render Men Immortal."

Savory—Satureja family, under Mercury; the winter variety is Satureja montana, a perennial and not as strongly flavored as Satureja hortensis, the summer annual. Culpeper says, "The juice, dropped into the eyes, cleareth a dull sight . . . heated with a little oil of roses, and dropped into the ears, easeth them of the noise and singing in them." According to Gerard, "Sommer Savorie doth marvelously prevaile against winde: therefore it is with good success boiled and eaten with beanes, peasons, and other windie pulses."

For flavoring, summer savory is an agreeable addition to meat sauces, stews, and poultry stuffing. The Germans, who call it Bohnenkraut, prefer it cooked with beans.

Sorrel—Rumex family, under Venus, is a perennial and does best in acid soil. Although rather coarse, it is of good use in giving a tang to salads and herb sandwiches and to a sauce for veal. It is a cooling herb, and Tournefort recommends sorrel to restore a decayed appetite. Medicinally its fame rests upon its reputation as a cure for scurvy. Carl Linnaeus mentions that sorrel and angelica are the only plants (except berries) used for food by the Laplanders. They boil it long in a copper kettle and then mix it with reindeer milk to form an acid whey. Preserved in wooden vessels, it is much relished by the Lapps. Leonhart Fuchs is said to have observed that when the flowers of wood sorrel are more than usually abundant, it presages a year of great rains. There is a French proverb that sorrel always grows with thistle, suggesting that the juice from the leaves of one is grateful for the stings of the other.

Sorrel Soup

A good handful of chopped sorrel leaves
Butter, size of an egg
1 cup boiling water
1 egg, separated
Salt to taste
1 pint milk
2 tablespoons cream
Bread

Heat the sorrel leaves with the butter until they are wilted. Add the boiling water and the egg white, well beaten. Then add the salt and permit the mixture to cook for an instant. Meanwhile, bring the milk to boiling point in a separate pan.

Lay pieces of thin bread in the bottom of a soup bowl. Pour over them the boiling sorrel, then add the milk. Last, blend in the egg yolk, slightly beaten and mixed with the cream. It is important that the soup not boil after the egg yolk is added.

Tarragon—Artemisia dracunculus, under Mars, is a perennial woody herb. It is difficult to establish in the north, where it dislikes the intense cold, and yet it is intolerant of being muffled up. This herb is indispensable in French cooking, where it is required in salads and omelets. The English associate it only with vinegar, which is good enough for winter use but the green leaves add a snap to lettuce salads and herb sandwiches that is distinctive.

To quote Evelyn, " 'Tis highly cordial and friendly to the Head, Heart, [and] Liver." Gerard relates that many strange tales have been told of tarragon; for example, if "the seed of flaxe [be] put into a radish roote or sea Onion, and so set, doth bring forth this herbe Tarragon." Perhaps the story grew from the fact that true, or French, tarragon seldom sets seed, and therefore propagation is obtained from cuttings, making the plant scarce.

French Omelet

Break into a bowl three eggs and beat with a fork. Add salt and pepper to taste. Next, add one teaspoon chopped parsley, one teaspoon chopped chives, and one and a half teaspoons chopped tarragon. Put butter the size of half an egg into a small frying pan and when hot, but not brown, add the omelet mixture and cook over a slow fire for two or three minutes. Fold and cook for one minute and serve. The omelet should not be very brown.

Thyme—Thymus family, under Venus, is a perennial. There are many varieties of thyme, and many are hardy in the north. The cooking sorts are little shrubs, and others, such as the wild or citrus thyme, are suitable for planting between stones or bricks in a path. Tournefort tells us that thyme was used by the ancients in their sacred ceremonies wherever they employed fire, but he gives no further explanation of this. Culpeper recommends thyme for various ills—of the lungs, for worms, dullness of sight, and even warts and frenzies. Parkinson advises combining thyme and rosemary with vinegar to be applied to the head for aches and as an aid for those who are troubled with lethargy. There are places in the Catskill Mountains where wild thyme grows and from which we have gathered our wild thyme honey, which is offered for its traditional virtue of promoting courage, besides the pleasure of enjoying the delicious flavor.

In cookery, thyme is almost a necessity, for it gives a fine flavor to meats, stuffings, and stews. To glorify the meatball, mix a pinch of fresh thyme, basil, savory, and sweet marjoram with the chopped meat.

SELECTED SOURCES

Abbott, Julia B. *Herbs and Plants Used for Medicinal Purposes by the Colonial Settlers*, Vol 5. Doylestown, PA: Bucks County Historical Society, 1926.

Andrews, Edward D. *The Community Industries of the Shakers.* Albany: University of the State of New York, 1932.

Bardswell, Frances Anne. *The Herb-Garden.* London: A. & C. Black, 1911.

Barton, Benjamin Herbert, and Thomas Castle. T*he British Flora Medica: A History of the Medicinal Plants of Great Britain* (2 vols.). London: Chatto & Windus, 1877.

Buc'hoz, Pierre-Joseph. *The Toilet of Flora* (1779). Reprinted by Rosetta Clarkson. Falls Village, CT: Herb Grower Press, 1939.

Burroughs, John. *Signs and Seasons.* New York: Houghton, Mifflin, 1892.

Cooper, J. W. *The Experienced Botanist or Indian Physician, Being a New System of Practice Founded on Botany.* Lancaster: John Bear, Printer, 1840.

Culpeper, Nicholas. *Complete Herbal.* London: Richard Evans, 1813.

Earle, Alice Morse. *Home Life in Colonial Days.* New York: Macmillan, 1898.

Earle, Alice Morse. *Old Time Gardens.* New York: Macmillan, 1901.

Evelyn, John. *Acetaria: A Discourse of Sallets*. London: B. Tooke Printers, 1699.

Gerard, John. *The Herball or Generall Historie of Plantes*. London: Adam Norton and Richard Whitaker, Printers 1633.

Gilmore, Melvin Randolph. U*ses of the Plants by the Indians of the Missouri Region*. Thirty-Third Annual Report of the Bureau of American Ethnology, Washington, DC, 1911–1912.

The Grete Herball. London: Peter Treveris, Printer, 1526.

Grieve, Maude. *A Modern Herbal*. New York: Harcourt, Brace, 1931.

Hale, Sarah Josepha, Ed. *Letters of Madame De Sevigne*, Vol. 7. New York: Mason Brothers, 1856.

Hedrick, Ulysses Prentiss. *A History of Agriculture in the State of New York*. Albany: New York State Agricultural Society, 1933.

The Holy Bible. Philadelphia: W. H. Harding, 1862.

Leyel, Mrs. C. F. *The Magic of Herbs: A Modern Book of Secrets*. London: Jonathan Cape, 1932.

Meighn, Moira. *A Little Booke of Conceited Secrets and Delightes for Ladies*. London: Medici Society, 1929.

Newton, James. *A Complete Herbal*. London: E. Cave at St. John's Gate, 1752.

Parkinson, John. *Theatrum Botanicum or The Theater of Plantes*. London: Thomas Cotes, 1640.

Pomet, Pierre A. A *Compleat History of Druggs* (English translation). London: J. and J. Bonwicke, 1737.

Porcher, Francis Peyre, M.D. *Resources of the Southern Fields and Forests, Medical, Economical and Agricultural*. Charleston: Walker, Evans & Cogswell, 1869.

Robinson, Matthew. *The New Family Herbal*. Wakefield: W. Nicholson & Sons, 1863.

Rohde, Eleanour Sinclair. *A Garden of Herbs*. Boston: Medici Society, 1922.

Rohde, Eleanour Sinclair. *The Old World Pleasaunce*. New York: Dial Press, 1925.

Shakespeare, William. The *Works of William Shakespeare in Ten Volumes*. New York: Bigelow, Smith, 1909.

Stearns, Samuel. *The American Herbal*. Walpole, NH: Thomas & Thomas, 1801.

Stockberger, W. W. *Drug Plants Under Cultivation*. US Department of Agriculture Farmers' Bulletin No. 663, 1915.

Thornton, Robert John, M.D. *A New Family Herbal*. London: Printed for Richard Phillips, 1810.

Tournefort, Joseph Pitton de. *The Compleat Herbal or The Botanical Institutions of Mr. Tournefort*. London: R. Bonwicke, 1719.

Turner, William. *A New Herball*. London: Steven Mierdman, 1551.

Tusser, Thomas. *Five Hundred Pointes of Good Husbandrie* (1580). London: Trübner & Co. for The English Dialect Society, 1878.

Wilder, Louise Beebe. *The Fragrant Path: A Book About Sweet Scented Flowers and Leaves*. New York: Macmillan, 1932.

INDEX

A
Abbott, Miss Julia, 29
Acetaria: A Discourse of Sallets (Evelyn), 16
acorns, 23
Aelius Gelenus, 43
alchemy, 15
Allium (onion), 48
aloes, 21
Anethum graveolens (dill), 45
angelica, 20, 42, 52
anise, 20
Anthriscus cerefolium (chervil), 44
aphrodisiac: herb Paris, 20
aphrodisiac: sage, 50
apple, 23, 41
  Balsam apple, 30
apple mint, 47
Apuleius Madaurensis, Lucius, 20
arbutus, 24, 38
Art Students League, 11
Artemisia, 41
Artemisia dracunculus (tarragon), 53
Artemisia vulgaris (mugwort), 22
As True as the Barnacle Tree, 7, 9
asthma, remedy for, 50
astringents, 30
astrological influences, 15
"Aunt Phoebe" (in Mink Hollow), 38

B
baldness, remedies for, 22, 48
balm, 22
  bee balm, 41
Balsam apple, 30
Barnacle Tree, 16, 17
Barrère, Georges, 7
Bartram, John, 24, 28, 29
basil, 10, 21, 29, 42, 43, 44, 54
beans, 23, 28, 51
bearberry, 24
bee balm, 41
beer making, 30
berries, 23, 24, 36, 37, 52
Bible, references to herbs in, 9, 15, 21
bittersweet, 20
black cohosh, 24
Blanch, Arnold, 12
Blanch, Lucile, 12
blood flow, staunching of, 27–28
blood purifiers, 30
blood toners, 37

bloodroot, 24
"blue-blows-stuff" (gentian), 39
blue borage, 44
Bohnenkraut (summer savory), 51
boneset, 24, 30, 37
Booth, Betsey, 38–40
borage, 21, 42, 44
Borago officinalis (borage), 44
bruises, treatments for, 29, 38
Bullard, Mrs. Marion, 7
burdock, 30
Bureau of American Ethnology, 26
burial spices, 30
burns, treatment for, 27
bush basil, 43

C
calamus, 21
calomel, 38
cardinal flowers, 26
Carey, Mr. and Mrs. Leon, 7
Carlson, John F., 11
carrot, wild, 26, 30
cascara sagrada, 28
Cashdollar, Mr. and Mrs. Albert, 7
cassia, 9, 15
castoreum, 21
catnip, 29, 38, 39
cattail flag root, 25
cedria, 18
chamomile, 22, 29, 41
Chase, William Merritt, 11
Chaste Making Tree, 18
cherries, 23
chervil, 42, 44, 46
Chief Observer, AMS as, 12–13
chinquapins, 23
chives, 29, 41, 42, 44, 48, 53
"Cholera Syrup," 40
cinchona, 24
cinnamon, 9, 15, 21, 45
cinquefoil, 30
citrus thyme, 53
cockerel, 38
coffee made from rye, 37
Cogswellia daucifolia (wild carrot), 26
colds, treatments for, 29–30, 38
columbine, 26
comfrey, 29
The Compleat Herbal or The Botanical Institutions of M. Tournefort, 8
coneflower, 26–27
Consumptive Syrup, 38
Cooper, Mr. and Mrs. Ashley, 11
coriander, 42
corn, 23, 28
Coronarius (rosemary), 49
costmary, 42
cough remedies, 18, 44, 49
Cramer, Florence Ballin, 7
Cramer, Konrad, 7
cramps, remedy for, 18
cranberries, 23
Crocus sativus, 21
Crolius, 18
croup, remedies for, 38
Crowfeet, 20
cucumber, Indian, 24
cudweed, 24–25
Culpeper, Nicholas, 8, 15, 18, 43, 46, 49, 50, 51, 54
cumin, 15, 20, 42, 45

D
Daily Freeman (Kingston), 7
dandelions, 30
Datura stramonium (jimsonweed), 19, 30

dill, 23, 42, 45
dock, 18, 30
doctrine of signatures, 26
dogwood, 30
Dragon Tree, 17
Dumarest, Father Noël, 28
dysentery, remedies for, 39

E
elm, 36
English Physician and Complete Herbal (Culpeper), 8
epilepsy, cure for, 18
Euonymus atropurpureus, 28
Euphrosium (borage), 44
Evelyn, John, 15–16, 45, 48, 50–51, 53
evil spirits, 20, 25, 33–36
eyesight. *See* sight, enhancement of

F
fatigue, herbs for, 25
fennel, 8, 42, 45, 48
fertility aid, 37
fever, remedies for, 39
feverfew, 24
fines herbes, 44
flax, 23, 41, 53
Foeniculum vulgare (fennel), 45
Fountain Tree, 17
foxglove, 30
frankincense, 15, 21
French omelet, 44, 53
French sorrel, 41–42
frenzies, remedies for, 54
Fuchs, Leonhart, 52

G
garlic, 48
gentian, 24, 39
Gerard, John, 8, 16–17, 18, 20, 22, 24, 44, 46, 48, 49, 51, 53
Gilmore, M. R., 26–27
ginseng, 26, 36–37
glycine apios (Indian "potatoes"), 24
golden seal, 38
gourd, 8, 26
gravel weed (arbutus), 38
The Grete Herball, 20–21, *22*

H
H. J. Heinz, 10
Hamburg parsley, 48–49
Hanson Studio, 11
headache, remedy for, 54
heartsease, 30
heat, insensitivity to, 26–27
hemp, 19, 25
henbane, 19, 25
Herald Tribune (New York), 10
The Herball or Generall Historie of Plantes (Gerard), 8, 16
herb garden, plan for, 41–42
"herb of grace" (rue), 30
Herb Lady of the Catskills, AMS as, 2, 10
herb Paris ("True Love"), 20
herb sandwich, 44, 46, 48, 52, 53
herb vinegar, 48
Herba amoris, 17
Hervey, Wilna, 7
hiccoughs, remedy for, 45
Historical Society of Woodstock, 11
"History and Hearsay" (AMS), 11. *See also Woodstock History and Hearsay* (AMS)
Hollerius (French physician), 43
Holy Basil of the Hindus, 10
hominy soup, 28

horehound, 30, 42
hound's tongue, 19
hyssop, 9, 15

I
Indian "potatoes," 24
Indian cucumber, 24
Indian garden, *27*
Indian hemp (henbane), 25
Indian quinine (gentian), 24
Indian turnip, 24
inflammation, remedies for, 30
"Isabella" (Keats), 10

J
jack in the pulpit, 24
Jackie Playboy Smith (AMS's Scottie), 7
jimsonweed, 24, 30
Joe-Pye weed (boneset), 24
Johannes (possessed man), 33–35
joint stiffness, remedy for, 18
juleps, 47

K
Katshrana, 28
Keats (John), 10
kidney ailments, 30, 37, 38

L
lavender, 29, 41
Leaycraft, Julia, 12
Lee, Mother Ann, 32
lethargy, remedy for, 54
licorice, 38
life everlasting, 24–25
Linnaeus, Carl, 52
live-forever, 30
lobelia, 24
Longfellow (Henry Wadsworth), 25
Louis XIV, 49
lovage, 42
love charms, 21, 24, 26
love philters, 19–20

M
madder roots, 18
Magee, Rosie, 11, 12
magnesium, 24
maize, 23
mandragora, 16, *19*, 19–20, 26
mandrake, 9, 15, 20, 24
maple bark, 37
maple syrup, 23, 38
Marjerome, 18
marjoram, 29, 41, 46, 48
  pot marjoram (oregano), 45
  sweet marjoram, 46, 54
Maverick Press, 9
mayapple, 30, 37–38
Medeola virginiana, 23–24
medicinal attributes of herbs, 17–18
medicine men, 24, 25–26, 28
melancholy, lightening of, 25–26, 41, 50
Mentha requienii (mint), 46
mescal bean, 19
mescaline (peyote), 26
milkweed, 24
Milne, Frieda (sister of AMS), 11–12
  mint, 10, 21, 22, 29, 41, 46, 46–47. *See also* peppermint; spearmint
mistletoe, 20
Mizaldus, 43
Momordica balsamina (Balsam apple), 30
mugwort, 22

mullein leaves, 37
Mumia, 18
"Mumme," 18
myrrh, 15, 21

N
narcotic properties, 19, 26
Nepeta mussinii, 41
nerves, soothing of, 22, 39
niter, 18
nutmeg, 41

O
Ocimum basilicum (basil), 43
Ocimum sanctum (holy basil), 43
omelet, 44, 53
onion, 38, 48
  sea onion, 53
orange mint, 47
oregano, 45–46
Origanum majorana (sweet marjoram), 46
Origanum vulgare (Pot Marjoram), 45
The Overlook, 12

P
palsies, remedy for, 18
Panax, 37
Parkinson, John, 17, 18, 24, 27–28, 44, 45, 46, 48, 54
parsley, 29, 38, 42, 44, 48–49, 53
parsnip, 21
"Patron Saint of the Salads" (John Evelyn), 15
peach, 24
peas, 23, 24
Pedanius Dioscorides, 43
Pelargoniuim crispum, 41
pennyroyal, 21, 30, 38
peppermint, 41, 47
Petroselinum crispum (parsley), 48
peyote, 26
physic garden, 29, 31
Physicians of Myddrai, 43
Pilgrims, 29
plantain leaves, 38
Pliny the Elder, 17, 20, 22, 43, 44, 46, 49
plum, 23
poison ivy, remedy for, 37
poppy seed, 8
Pot Marjoram (oregano), 45
potatoes, 23
  Indian "potatoes," 24
potpourri recipes, 8–9
poultices, 30, 38, 48
The Press and Sun-Bulletin (Binghamton), 10
puffballs, 37
pumpkins, 23
purple basil, 10

Q
Quakers, 9, 11, 23, 24, 29–30, 32
quinces, 22
quinsy, remedy for, 24

R
radish, 48, 53
rampion, 42
Ranunculus aquatilis (Crowfeet), 20
rheumatism, remedies for, 30, 37
rice, 23
rocket, 20
root parsley, 48–49
rose, 8, 31–32, 41
rose water, 31

rosemary, 21, 41, 48, 49–50, 54
Rosmarinus officinalis (rosemary), 49
rue, 9, 15, 20, 30, 41, 50
Rumex family (sorrel), 51
rush, 37
Russian mint, 47
rye, 37

S
saffron, 21
sage, 22, 29, 38, 39, 50–51
Salvia officinalis (sage), 50
sandwiches, 44, 46, 48, 52, 53
sarsaparilla, 24
sassafras, 24, 30, 38, 40
Satureja hortensis (summer savory), 51
Satureja montana (winter savory), 51
savory, 29, 42, 46, 51, 54
Scythian Lamb, 17
Sensitive Plant, 17
sesame, 8
The Shaker Manifesto, 31
Shakers, 9, 30–32
Shakespeare (William), 20
shallots, 48
sheep sorrel, 38
Shotwell, James T., 13
Shultis, Mrs. (local farming woman), 11
sight, enhancement of, 21, 45, 51, 54
"simples," 25–26, 30, 38
sleep, promotion of, 17, 38, 44
smartweed, 30
Smith, Anita M. (AMS)
  and *As True as the Barnacle Tree*, 7, 9
  early days in Woodstock, 11–13
  hearing local tales, 35, 37–38
  Herb Lady of the Catskills, 10
  Quaker ancestors of, 23
  and Stonecrop Garden & Shop, 7, 8–10, 12
  and story of Johannes, 33
  and *Woodstock History and Hearsay*, 1, 9
  Woodstock's Chief Observer, 12–13
Smith, Lucy Pancoast, 11
Society of Friends. *See* Quakers
"The Song of Hiawatha" (Longfellow), 25–26
soft horehound, 42
sorrel, 51–52
  sheep sorrel, 38
Sorrowful Tree, 17
soup
  consommé, 46
  hominy, 28
  sorrel, 52
  tomato, 44
Southern New York and Connecticut Antique Show, 10
spearmint, 8, 26, 38, 39, 42, 47
Speicher, Elsie, 7
Speicher, Eugene, 7
spicewood, 30
spikenard, 21, 24, 30
squawroot (black cohosh), 24
squill, 20
Steele, Zulma, 12
Stonecrop Garden & Shop, 7–10, *39, 42, 47, 51, 54*
  origins of, 9–10, 12
sumac, 24
summer savory, 51
sunflowers, 23
sweet basil, 43

sweet cicely (chervil), 44
sweet fern, 37, 39
sweet geraniums, 41
sweet marjoram, 46, 54
Symphytum officinale, 29

T
tansy, 30, 42
tarragon, 42, 44, 48, 53
Theatrum Botanicum (Parkinson), 17
thistle, 52
thyme, 21, 29, 41, 53–54
Thymus family (thyme), 53
tobacco, 23, 26, 49
tomato soup, 44
tonics, 24, 28, 37
Toonerville Trolley silent films, 7
Tournefort, Joseph Pitton de, 8, 24, 44, 45, 49, 50, 52, 53–54
Treveris, Peter, 21
"True Love" (herb Paris), 20
Tulasi, 10, 43
turnip, Indian, 24

U
Ulster County Townsman, 7
Unguentum Sympatheticum, 18

V
valerian, 41
venom and poison, treatments for, 20, 46, 49, 50
verbena, 20, 31
vervain, 22
vinegar, 38, 44, 45, 48, 53, 54
violets, white, 41
Vishnu, Ocimum sanctum consecrated to, 43

W
Wagner, Mrs. (of Willow), 38
wahoo, 28
warts, remedy for, 54
watercress, 42
white ash, 20
white violets, 41
White, Hervey, 9
wild carrot, 26, 30
wild gourd, 26
wild thyme, 54
wintergreen, 24, 30, 36
witch doctors, 35
witch hazel, 24, 35, 36
witches and witchcraft, 11, 19, 19–20, 20, 28, 30, 35
WKNY (Kingston), 9
wood sorrel, 52
woodbine, 37
Woodstock History and Hearsay (AMS), 13
Woodstock Library Fair, 13
wormwood, 9, 15, 38
wounds, treatment for, 18, 27, 29, 37

Y
yarrow, 26, 37
yellow dock, 30

Z
Zethy, Simeon, 43

ABOUT THE AUTHOR

Anita M. Smith (1893–1968) was born a Quaker in Philadelphia. In 1912, she came to Woodstock to study painting at the Art Students League Summer School. Her teachers included John F. Carlson and Frank DuMond. Soon, she was exhibiting her work at the National Academy of Design, the Art Institute of Chicago, and the Pennsylvania Academy of the Fine Arts. In 1934, she built a bluestone home near the intersection of Rock City Road and Glasco Turnpike and embarked on a second career as a herbalist. In 1937, she joined the fledgling Herb Society of America, and by 1940, her business—with customers throughout the country—was one of four such enterprises on the East Coast. She began contributing papers to the Historical Society of Woodstock at this time. Just as she had designed her gardens with an artist's eye, Smith captured the landscape in her writing. In the 1950s, she wrote the town's first history. A blend of local legends, personal anecdotes, and scholarship, *Woodstock History and Hearsay* was published in 1959. Anita Smith also wrote *The Landscape of History* and *The Quest of Abel Knight: The Quakers and Shakers.*